Adventure

THE VALUE OF *RISK* IN CHILDREN'S PLAY

by Joan Almon

Alliance for Childhood

Contents

Alliance for Childhood
P.O. Box 5758
Annapolis, MD 21403
202-643-8242
www.allianceforchildhood.org

© photosearch.com

Introduction

To play is to risk; to risk is to play.[1]

— Diane Ackerman

Risk has become a four-letter word in the U.S.—something to protect children from at all costs. Yet children throughout the ages played freely in the outdoors with their peers, usually without adult supervision once they reached a certain age. They took on as much adventure as they felt ready for. Injuries occurred, but when we have asked adults to review their play memories, they can think of few children they knew who suffered any serious harm. Bumps and bruises, yes, and even an occasional broken arm or leg, but rarely anything worse than that. And while no one wants to see a child injured, the benefits of experiencing risk need to be weighed against the harm done by never learning to cope with it. The latter can be truly dangerous.

Facing risk helps children assess the world around them and their place in it. Children love to see how high they can climb on a ladder, a tree, or a jungle gym. Over time they see their abilities grow, and they become ever more confident about stretching their boundaries and taking appropriate chances. They also learn about their limits and the consequences of going too far beyond their limits. As they grow older they apply these lessons in a variety of real life situations.

It is time to rethink risk and see its benefits as well as its difficulties. Not long ago, after all, "play" was also viewed as a four-letter word and widely disparaged. Then articles began to appear in major newspapers and magazines; films featuring play were aired on public television, and public opinion began to shift.[2] Contributing to the change in outlook about play are the many recent studies documenting the value of play. The *European Early Childhood Education Research Journal* began a recent editorial with these words: "The proliferation of the number of studies on play in the past decade is remarkable and an interesting cultural phenomenon by itself." It

goes on to say, "The various benefits of play for children are beyond doubt, which is supported by an interesting number of empirical studies."[3]

Despite so much attention to play, there is still much to be done to restore it to childhood, including in early education. Surveys indicate that today's children have far less outdoor playtime than their parents did, and that the vast majority of parents recognize this as a problem. They want children to have greater opportunities for play, but urban parents, in particular, express a need for supervision of the children while they are outside playing.[4] It is vitally important that these issues be addressed. However, it is also time to redeem "risk" and make it an acceptable part of childhood again.

Yet allowing—and even encouraging—children to engage in adventurous play poses a problem. How do children learn to risk-assess if adults are always present and doing it for them? The Alliance for Childhood found one solution in the profession of playwork in the United Kingdom. Playworkers understand the nature of play and help create spaces for play. But they hold back from directing children's play or even intervening with it unless it is clearly called for. Playwork is described in more detail throughout this publication.

Any adult encouraging children's play needs to differentiate between extreme risk and reasonable risk. For example, one would not let a three-year-old play with an open flame, but one does teach scouts how to build campfires in safe and secure ways. It is not fire per se that is the danger, but a lack of understanding of its risks and how to manage them. Likewise one would not want a six-year-old to cross a log that is stretched over a deep ravine. But learning to cross a log over a stream that does not have a dangerous drop-off is a regular part of the lives of elementary-age children who play freely in the outdoors. In other words, not all risks are the same. Much depends on the age, experiences, and cognitive and physical abilities of the child, as well as the potential consequences of an accident.

Overall, there are reasonable risks for children of certain ages and abilities to take, and there are more extreme risks that can cause serious injuries and even death. Three levels of risk are identified in Chapter Two. As children develop skills through play, they can master more complex challenges. But individual differences in children's skill development and assessment of risk during play differ widely across chronological periods. Fortunately, most children have an innate ability to assess risk, as we discuss in this publication. With opportunity to practice they become skilled in taking risks. *Opportunity to master increasingly challenging play is essential for safety in play.*

This publication is intended as an introduction to the topic of adventurous play and risk. It is not a detailed guide for understanding risk for every age group or circumstance. More detailed guides on this topic are definitely needed.

We begin, in Chapter One, with a discussion of why it is so urgent to continue restoring active play in children's lives. That chapter provides the fundamental context for understanding the essential role of risk in play and why children need a free-ranging childhood.

In Chapter Two, we describe developmentally appropriate risk in play and why it is so important. Chapter Three looks at how risk in play is handled in adventure playgrounds, both here and abroad. Chapter Four explores the relatively low rates of injuries associated with adventure playgrounds, and Chapter Five looks at basic ways to assess risk in play settings. Finally, Chapter Six brings in the voices of children and suggests next steps.

Throughout, we include results from a survey of play experts and adventure-playground directors. It was commissioned by the Alliance for Childhood and conducted by Halcyon Reese-Learned, Ph.D., who was Executive Director of the Houston Adventure Play Association for three years, beginning in 1992. The Association conducted observational research on, and ran, three adventure playgrounds—two on Houston public school campuses and one at a Houston Parks and Recreation site.

Adventure playgrounds are relatively rare in the U.S. but plentiful in other countries. It is difficult to find solid statistics on the playgrounds, but several web sites state that there are about 1,000 adventure playgrounds in Europe, particularly in Scandinavia, Switzerland, France, Germany, the Netherlands, and the United Kingdom. Japan has a significant number, as well.[5]

Adventure playgrounds contain varying levels of risk ranging from sand, water, and zip lines to construction zones where children build two- and three-story huts with hammers and nails. The greater the risk level, the more likely the playground will be staffed by playworkers. The playgrounds are primarily frequented by children from five to 12 or 14 years of age. They are described in some detail throughout this publication. A delightful film showing scenes from an adventure playground in England is available on YouTube.[6]

Adventure playgrounds generally foster more risk than conventional playgrounds. They also keep some records on accident rates, lawsuits, insurance issues, and related matters. They provide a sort of laboratory setting for understanding risk in children's play.

> **Halcyon Reese-Learned's research counters a number of common myths. For example, contrary to popular assumptions:**
>
> ◆ Risky play—in contrast to hazardous play— does *not* lead to high accident rates.
>
> ◆ Parks districts that have adventure playgrounds are *not* beset with lawsuits.
>
> ◆ Parks districts that have adventure playgrounds do *not* pay higher insurance rates.

We have also gathered and listed in the back resources from the U.S. and abroad that shed light on the benefits of risk and risk management, as well as information on play and playwork. There are also extensive endnotes that provide valuable resources.

We hope this publication will help professionals, parents, and the broader public become more understanding of children's need for developmentally appropriate risk in play—and more confident about offering them opportunities for dealing with risk.

CHAPTER ONE
Restoring Active Play to Childhood

It could be argued that active play is so central to child development that it should be included in the very definition of childhood.[7]

— American Academy of Pediatrics

Allowing children to experience risk in play means allowing them to play freely and meet the world on their own terms through play. All of this requires that play becomes an active part of children's lives again. In the following chapters, we will focus directly on the subject of risk. But here, in this chapter, we want to first ground our entire discussion in a firm understanding of how essential active play of all kinds is for healthy childhood development and how threatened it remains. Only if we're serious about restoring active play will we be able to also address children's need to learn to assess and manage developmentally appropriate risks in play.

Experts in play widely agree that today's children in the U.S. have far fewer opportunities for free play than did previous generations. This is backed up by research by Sandra Hofferth and others.[8] A combination of factors has driven play out of childhood: Children spend long hours with electronic media each day; they engage in many adult-organized activities; schools have reduced or eliminated recess; and adults experience high levels of fear regarding stranger danger and play injuries.

Fortunately, there are some recent indicators that public opinion about play is shifting. Parents are indicating that they want their children to play more, but they want them to have some supervision.[9] A number of play and nature organizations, health officials, city planners, policy makers, and others have begun working together in the U.S. Play Coalition[10] and in local coalitions to restore play. Over 500 cities recently applied for recogni-

tion as a Playful City in KaBOOM!'s Playful Cities USA program; 217 were accepted.[11] These cities are committed to creating more and better opportunities for play. Participants in the Playful Cities range from grassroots groups to mayors. Also, some excellent films and short videos, books, and articles have appeared in recent years promoting the benefits of play. See the Resources list in this publication for a sample of materials.

There is also a renewed focus on active play as a result of the nation's concerns about childhood obesity. First Lady Michelle Obama's "Let's Move!"[12] campaigns are important efforts in this regard.

Currently, a growing wave of attention is focusing on the need to restore recess in elementary schools. Some schools or districts actually have official policies against recess, often citing the need for more class time to raise test scores. In other cases schools have recess, but it is withheld from individual children or classes as a punishment. A 2010 review of eight recess studies by the Centers for Disease Control and Prevention concludes that:

> School boards, superintendents, principals, and teachers can feel confident that providing recess to students on a regular basis may benefit academic behaviors, while also facilitating social development and contributing to overall physical activity and its associated health benefits. There was no evidence that time spent in recess had a negative association with cognitive skills, attitudes, or academic behavior.[13]

This view was underscored by the American Academy of Pediatrics, which issued a policy statement at the end of 2012 called "The Crucial Role of Recess in School." It states:

> Recess is at the heart of a vigorous debate over the role of schools in promoting the optimal development of the whole child. A growing trend toward reallocating time in school to accentuate the more academic subjects has put this important facet of a child's school day at risk. Recess serves as a necessary break from the rigors of concentrated, academic challenges in the classroom. But equally important is the fact that safe and well-supervised recess offers cognitive, social, emotional, and physical benefits that may not be fully appreciated when a decision is made to diminish it. Recess is unique from, and a complement to, physical education—not a substitute for it. The American Academy of Pediatrics believes that recess is a crucial and necessary component of a child's development and, as such, it should not be withheld for punitive or academic reasons.[14]

In addition, the National Wildlife Federation is running a campaign called Ranger Rick Restores Recess,[15] and a resource sheet called "Take a Stand on Recess" has been developed by the Providence Children's Museum.[16] Currently, the U.S. Play Coalition is preparing a report summarizing play research and giving recommendations for restoring recess.[17]

The nature of play

Play is the way children discover themselves—starting with their fingers and toes and gradually including their whole body, their emotions, and their minds. In play, the whole child is engaged. There is probably no other activity that integrates children as fully as does play.

Play is also the way children discover the world around them. They explore, invent, and transform it to

Photo: Paige Salmon, Courtesy of Roger Williams Park Zoo

suit their needs. Cut off play and a wide range of children's abilities never fully develop. Play-deprived children fail to know themselves and the world around them with the depth available to the playful child.

Play also serves the important purpose of showing children that life can be fun even though it is often rich with difficulties. Children use play to lower stress levels and cope with life's challenges. Children also work hard at play. They have ideas and they go to great lengths to carry them out—over shorter periods when they are very young, and over days and weeks when they are of school age.

Many people confuse play with activities run by adults, such as sports. While sports offer some real benefits for children—especially when adult-led instruction and competition do not begin too early—it is not the children who are setting the rules and changing them as needed, it is the adults. In play, children work together to change the rules to meet the situation they face, which is a powerful social experience.

Many people also see video games as a form of play. They point out that children are given a range of options for interaction. That is true, but the range itself is set by the creators of the game and not by the children. The adults create the general story line and the choices are created by the adults. In real play the children create the story line and the options are as limitless as their imaginations.

Similarly, children create whatever dress-ups or structures they need for their play out of the simplest materials at hand—sticks and stones, cloths and ropes, hammers and nails. They especially love materials thrown away by adults for they are then very free to use them as they see fit. They reuse the same basic play materials for numerous scenarios, exercising endless creativity and innovation. In contrast, sports and video games require equipment that is purchased, often at great expense, so children need to be careful with it. Furthermore, the equipment is specialized and has limited uses, unlike open-ended play materials.

What then is "real play"? Basically it involves children creating their own stories and directing their own activities. Playworkers in the U.K., those wonderful, quirky individuals who support children's play without directing or dominating it, have an interesting way of describing play. First of all, they say it cannot be defined. It is too vast. They liken it to love, which touches every aspect of human life but refuses to fit into a neat definition. Play can be described, however, and they describe it this way:

"Play is a set of behaviors that are freely chosen, personally directed, and intrinsically motivated."[18]

In other words, play ideas bubble up from within children themselves, not to meet an external goal but to satisfy their own needs. Children then choose how to play out their ideas. They direct and change the play scenarios as needed. The end result is usually a rich and deeply satisfying experience.

Play is fundamental to healthy development

Play is so fundamental to human life that it survives even in very difficult circumstances, such as those portrayed in an on-line "postcard" called "The Dumps, Train Tracks and Polluted Water Where Kids Play."[19]

Joe Frost, professor emeritus at the University of Texas at Austin's College of Education, examined

> *In play, children work together to change the rules to meet the situation they face, which is a powerful social experience.*

research studies that looked at accounts of play among enslaved children, victims of war, extreme poverty, and natural disasters. His conclusion:

> Contemporary studies of natural and other man-made disasters show that play and some forms of work are therapeutic, helping children understand and cope with traumatic circumstances—diminishing the trauma inflicted by brutality or extreme destitution. Children play even under the harshest conditions, and most slave children were not exceptions, though after the first four or five years of their childhood work dominated their lives.[20]

Likewise, a study by George Eisen, Director of the Institute for Regional and International Studies at California Polytechnic University in Pomona, concludes from documents recording instances of children's play during the Holocaust that children did play in the ghettos and concentration camps. Many of their games reflected the gruesome realities of their lives. Play was a way of coping with terrible realities, but it was also a way of escaping, for however short a period, from those realities. A survivor of the Warsaw ghetto is quoted by Eisen as saying:

> When I am in play, I forget my hunger. I forget that outside are such evil Germans even existing. Early in the morning I rush to the child care center, and I wish that the day would never end, because when it is getting dark, we all have to return home. In my room it is so full of dark shadows and black fear.

A play intervention in a Romanian hospital in 2000 also demonstrates that the fundamental urge to play survives and can be revived even when play deprivation is extreme. Playwork educators Fraser Brown and Sophie Webb of Leeds Metropolitan University in England engaged in a small-scale study that tracked what happened when playworkers began working with 16 abandoned children in a Romanian pediatric hospital. The children had lived there for years. Lack of staff resulted in the children, ages 1 to 10 years, being tied to their cots for most of the day. The playworkers took the children out of their beds for a period of time each day and helped them to play—including, in this extreme case, providing the kind of "cuddling" playworkers decided was necessary to help children prepare to play. This therapeutic playwork project was the only change in the children's circumstances that occurred, yet the results were very visible, as Brown and Webb describe:

> … the children changed dramatically. Their social interaction became more complex; physical activity showed a distinct move from gross to fine motor skills; the children's understanding of the world around them was improved; and they began to play in highly creative ways. They no longer sat rocking, staring vacantly into space. Instead they had become fully engaged active human beings.[21]

This play intervention occurred because of the great concern of the newly appointed director of the hospital. Most of the children benefited from the intervention. Fourteen of the 16 were later adopted or placed in foster homes. The researchers added, however, that "sadly, the other two were eventually transferred to a children's mental hospital."[22]

It is inspiring to know that play can be restored even when it's been seriously suppressed. It is like a spring in nature that is clogged with debris but which flows freely once the sticks, stones, and leaves that block it are removed. The urge to play may be blocked and seem to have disappeared, but with effort—sometimes small and sometimes considerable—the blockages can be removed and the life of play begins again. This seems to be true in adulthood, as well as in childhood, according to anecdotal reports from professors of play and early childhood courses, who help their students who did not grow up with free play to develop the capacity for it.

> *The urge to play is so fundamental to human life that it survives even in very difficult circumstances.*

Children need freedom to play

Just a few decades ago, most children in the U.S. grew up playing freely outdoors, riding their bikes, and walking to school. Unfortunately, children have fewer and fewer opportunities for such play, especially during their elementary school years, a time when many children used to roam freely in their neighborhoods and play in a wide range of ways with their friends.

In general, British children today seem to have more freedom to play than their counterparts in the U.S. Yet a study released there in January 2013 showed that only 25% of primary school children in England are allowed to travel home from school alone, compared with 86% in 1971.[23]

Fortunately, a movement to restore "free-range childhood" is growing in the U.S., sparked by Lenore Skenazy who allowed her nine-year-old son to travel home alone on a subway in New York City after he repeatedly requested permission to do this. She and her husband decided Izzy, their son, was ready, and she dropped him off at Bloomingdale's with a subway map, a MetroCard, a $20 bill, and several quarters, just in case he had to make a call. He returned to his home in Manhattan safe and sound as she expected. A month later she wrote about the incident in her column for *The New York Sun*.[24] A firestorm of media attention immediately followed, and she was quickly dubbed "America's worst mom." Later she wrote a humorous and insightful book, *Free-Range Kids*, and she's become a popular lecturer. Her point: Know your children, give them the freedom they can handle, and don't let your own fears get in the way. Lenore is sympathetic to parental fears—and readily admits she has many herself. But she encourages parents to become more savvy about risk assessment. And she does so with a delightful, acerbic wit.

> …a lot of parents today are really bad at assessing risk. They see no difference between letting their children walk to school and letting them walk through a firing range. When they picture their kids riding their bikes to a birthday party, they see them dodging Mack trucks with brake problems. To let their children play unsupervised in a park at age

eight or ten or even thirteen seems about as responsible as throwing them in the shark tank at Sea World with their pockets full of meatballs.

Any risk is seen as too much risk. A crazy, not-to-be-taken, see-you-on-the-local-news risk. And the only thing these parents don't seem to realize is that the greatest risk of all just might be trying to raise a child who never encounters *any* risks.[25]

Some helpful tips on free-range parenting have also been compiled by the Appalachian Mountain Club, which recommends:

♦ Turn off the TV so you don't get an overdose of bad news.

♦ Counter "worst-first" thinking with real-world numbers.

♦ Let children play together without you around.

♦ Give children opportunities to practice self-regulation.

♦ Create communities that support free-range children.[26]

Health and play

In the past one often saw children outside playing and rarely saw an obese child. Today one rarely sees children engaged in outdoor play, in riding their bikes through neighborhoods—even very safe ones—or walking to school. At the same time, childhood obesity has become a national health issue. There are a number of factors that contribute to the obesity problem, including unhealthy food choices and a lack of access to healthy food options, a lack of exercise, and long hours spent sitting in front of screens. The absence of active play outdoors needs to be viewed as another important contributing factor.

As Joe Frost has noted, "setting aside enough time every day for appropriate play at school, along with healthy food choices, would be enough to shrink most children's expanding waistlines."[27]

How big is the problem? The Centers for Disease Control and Prevention state that over the past thirty years obesity among children ages 6 to 11 increased from 7% in 1980 to nearly 18% in 2010. Among adolescents aged 12 to19, the number of obese children more than tripled, from 5% to 18% during the same period.[28]

In 2007, the American Academy of Pediatrics issued a policy[29] calling for more play time for children and discussing the way that play enhances children's overall healthy development. In 2011 it revised the policy to more fully include the play needs of children in poverty.[30] In regard to obesity, the first statement notes: "In contrast to passive entertainment, play builds active, healthy bodies. In fact, it has been suggested that encouraging unstructured play may be an exceptional way to increase physical activity levels in children, which is one important strategy in the resolution of the obesity epidemic."[31]

But improved physical health is not the only value pediatricians see in play. Their general view is well represented by this statement: "Perhaps above all, play is a simple joy that is a cherished part of childhood."[32]

Photo courtesy of Stacy McReynolds, San Antonio Zoo

CHAPTER TWO

Understanding Risk and Its Role in Play

> *Risk: possibility of loss or injury; peril*
>
> — Merriam-Webster's Collegiate Dictionary,
> Eleventh Edition

Play stretches children's boundaries as they explore their world in ever deeper and wider ways. Such stretching inevitably brings some risk. Fortunately, children have an innate ability to assess risk. That allows them to sense risk and either back away from it if they feel unready to cope with it, or move forward, step by step, as they test their skills. For instance, watch children climb a tall step ladder and see them gauge how far they can go. The height varies according to age, developmental level, and ability, and over time children climb higher and higher.

The value of risk in play is frequently dismissed in the United States with quick responses about liability and insurance issues, as if that is the end of the subject. But other countries have probed more deeply and have developed more nuanced positions. In the United Kingdom, for example, a number of national organizations that are concerned with children's play have grouped together to form The Play Safety Forum. The Forum has produced a publication titled *Managing Risk in Play Provision: Implementation Guide*, which they summarize in this way:

> Children need and want to take risks when they play. Play provision aims to respond to these needs and wishes by offering children stimulating, challenging environments for exploring and developing their abilities. In doing this, play provision aims to manage the level of risk so that children are not exposed to unacceptable risks of death or serious injury.[33]

In providing opportunities for play and risks, it is helpful to identify several levels of risk. Often one is fearful that children will take extreme risks. But they rarely do unless they are training for an extreme sport, are egged on by peers as in "I double dare you," or have had too few opportunities to develop risk-assessment skills in adventurous play. We recognize risk as dividing into three basic levels.

1. Challenging activities. These look risky and take courage to do, but they come with plenty of safety features.

> *Examples:* Children's museums frequently have tall climbing structures that are two to three stories high in a central atrium. They are challenging but have nets all around so that a child cannot fall out of the structure.[34] For teens and adults, bungee jumping is an example. No skills are needed—just a brave heart and evidence that the company handling the bungee jumps takes safety seriously.

2. Moderate risk. Things could go wrong but generally don't, provided the child has experience in risk-assessment, and adult oversight is appropriate to the child's age and abilities.

> *Examples:* Zip lines designed for children, high climbing equipment, and building forts or playhouses with tools. Serious injuries can happen but rarely do if children have a sense of their own abilities and can risk assess.

3. Advanced/extreme risk. These activities require much practice and advanced skills.

Examples: Parkour[35] has become a popular activity during which teens and adults climb anything on their path, leaping from one place to another and trying not to touch the ground. When taken to extremes, participants leap from building to building, crossing wide divides. Other examples include advanced leaps with skateboards, motorcycle stunts (think Evel Knievel) and cliff diving. Many examples can be found on-line.[36]

In this publication we include risks at levels one and two, but are primarily concerned with level two—activities that provide children with genuine risk that they can assess for themselves and make choices about their level of participation. We think they are a necessary part of a child's development and without opportunities to practice taking calculated risks they will be ill-prepared to meet many of the challenges life offers.

What is reassuring is that while adventurous play brings some bumps and bruises, the rate of serious injury seems to be surprisingly low, as we discuss in Chapter Four regarding data about injuries. This does not mean adults should throw out their sense of caution regarding children. But they should examine their concerns to differentiate appropriate concerns from inappropriate fears. It is also important to differentiate between risks that are visible and which children can assess for themselves and hidden hazards, like broken or poorly designed equipment, which children are not aware of. The latter need to be detected and avoided, and that is the responsibility of adults.

While many parents fear exposing their children to risks, others report that it is a revelation to see that their children have an in-born survival instinct that is an efficient self-regulation system. For example, Danielle Marshall, who works at the play advocacy organization KaBOOM!, was struck by the careful monitoring of risk her six-month-old baby exercised. She recalled her own reading of the studies about the "visual cliff" by Gibson and Walk.[37] In this study, six-month-olds who could crawl were put on a large sheet of plexiglass with a checkerboard design underneath. As they crawled they came to a point where the checkerboard dropped by a foot or more, although the plexiglass stayed at the same level. The experiment was originally designed to test depth perception, but the researchers noticed something

more. Already at six months the babies recognized risk and showed an innate ability to risk-assess. They noticed the drop off and hesitated while deciding how to navigate it. Some retreated from the drop-off while others cautiously crawled forward, testing the edge to be sure they could not fall down. Danielle Marshall commented, "Now I've seen it with my own eyes. My daughter crawls to the edge of the bed and then stops."[38]

A similar observation was made by Jean Liedloff, author of *The Continuum Concept*.[39] In an interview with Michael Mendizza of Touch the Future,[40] she describes her experiences with native Amazon tribes in a thought-provoking way. A family she met

> … had dug a pit to get mud to make the walls of their house. Into the pit they had thrown branches and sharp sticks. It had rained and was partly filled with water. *Cananasiniawana* [their one-year-old child] was taking his first, clumsy steps. He would go to the edge of the pit and sit down and then stand up and fall on his bottom, but he would never fall into the pit. Whenever he fell it would be the other way.

> Puppy dogs and kittens don't appear to be falling somewhere on purpose, but they don't fall into the fire do they? They don't fall into the pool do they? We trust puppies and kittens not to burn themselves up in fires but we don't trust our own children.[41]

These examples raise important questions about risk. What is this innate ability we can observe in babies and young animals that keeps them from falling off the bed or into the pit? What is the parent's role in supporting the continuing development of children's ability to handle risk?

A beautiful example of such support is described by Alexandra Lopez Reitzes, a mother of two in New York. She writes that her partner, the father of her

As children grow, they embrace risk as a natural part of life and develop a finely tuned sense for risk assessment, an essential skill for survival.

children, "has scaled 50-foot rocks, paddled across the Hudson River to New Jersey and back, whittled with a pocket knife and used a drill press—all with our eight-year-old son."[42]

Another way to support children's play is to simply watch and see how they play and resolve conflict. By doing this, one can learn a great deal about the children, including how capable they are of handling their own play.

Matching risks with age and developmental stage

As children grow, they embrace risk as a natural part of life and develop a finely tuned sense for risk assessment, an essential skill for survival. If human beings had not learned to master risk we would have died out as a species long ago, given the myriad dangers of life in the wild, as well as in many urban settings.

Children typically test their limits as they climb trees, roll down hillsides, and run with abandonment. Watch the joy of a six-year-old as he confronts his fears of crossing the creek on a log. He is discovering that his sense of balance has developed to the point where he can manage something that was impossible a year before. He needs such opportunities in order to know his own ever-expanding abilities. And he does not mind failure. Children are prepared for bumps and scrapes, and even a broken bone does not stop them for long. They heal fast—generally much faster than adults. While children need protection from unacceptable hazards and extreme risks that can result in serious injury or death, they need ample opportunities to face reasonable risks when they are young.

In general, there is a more open attitude toward risk and adventurous play for children in the U.K. than in the U.S. Britain's Big Lottery Fund has spent hundreds of millions of pounds to refurbish and build playgrounds, including a large number of adventure playgrounds. Its 2012 report described the balance sought between safety and freedom in play:

> The programme encouraged risky play—which gave children the chance to engage in stimulating and adventurous play. This was often challenging but ultimately rewarding for children and young people, parents and play workers. Approaches to risky play included climbing, kayaking, rock pooling, fire play, play in the dark, play in the mud and all-weather play. Risky play required projects to strike a fine balance between responsibilities to keep children safe and giving freedom to children and young people to assess and manage their own level of risk. As a result parents and play workers became more open to the prospect of allowing children to engage in risky play activities and became more comfortable and confident with this approach to play. The programme has left a legacy enabling children to engage in play in more adventurous ways.[43]

In the U.S. we tend to confuse risk and hazards and try to protect children from both. Hazards are objects which children cannot see or be expected to avoid, while risks are those experiences and objects that are out in the

Photo: Paige Salmon, Courtesy of Roger Williams Park Zoo

open and obvious. Broken glass on a usually well-tended playground is a hazard that children are not expecting to find and don't think to avoid. Many play injuries are related to poorly designed or broken equipment. It is hard for children to assess the safety of equipment. That takes well-trained playground inspectors, who have special tools for measuring openings on equipment, for instance, to make sure that head entrapment cannot happen. But climbing high on a structure or hammering together a play house at an adventure playground provides risks that a child recognizes and chooses to encounter or avoid.

An article in *The New York Times* science section entitled "Can a Playground Be Too Safe?"[44] featured a very tall jungle gym in a New York playground. It also described a study by Norwegian researchers, Ellen Sandseter and Ellen Beate Hansen, who studied young children at play to see what types of risky play they gravitated to most often. They identified six categories: 1) Play with great heights; 2) Play with high speed; 3) Play with harmful tools; 4) Play near dangerous elements such as fire and water; 5) Rough-and-tumble play; and 6) Play where the children can disappear or get lost.[45]

© photosearch.com

Examples of play environments that encourage healthy risk-taking

Adventure playgrounds—which sprang up in Europe during and after World War II, and which can be found in the U.S. in small numbers, as well—offer a wide range of play opportunities that include most or all of the above-mentioned risk-taking activities. Typically they have water, sand, mud, zip lines, high sliding boards, climbing structures, and forts and houses built by the children with hammers, nails, and lumber. In European adventure playgrounds it is common to see a fire tended by an adult with help from school-age children. This can seem shocking at first to an American, but guidance in fire building was—and hopefully still is—a regular part of being a Girl or Boy Scout.

"What we like to say is that there are no hidden risks on the [adventure] playground," explains Denise Brown of the Berkeley Adventure Playground.[46] "Even a young child walking through the playground gates can look around and tell that it's a different type of playground, and there are sticks and boards and nails and rocks and things that they need to watch out for."[47]

Adventure playgrounds seek a balance between safety and freedom to play. They have guidelines and rules but try to make them appropriate. The web site for the Berkeley adventure playground spells out some of the rules of the playground. They include the following:[48]

- The playground is designed for children seven years old and older, however younger children are welcome as long as they are *within arm's reach* of a participating adult. No one under 6 should use the zip line.

- Everyone must wear sturdy shoes like tennis shoes, not flip-flops, sandals, crocs or clogs. Stepping on a nail is a possibility and sturdy shoes protect feet.

- Pick up the wood on the ground (which is a trip hazard) and put it in the wood racks. If it is naily wood put it in the red zones.

- Wear clothes that can get dirty, wet, and painted on. Consider bringing a change of clothes for wet or muddy days.

- Everyone needs to sign the walk-in waiver when you come in.

- Keep your cell phone in your pocket.

- Do not help children onto the wooden seat at the top of the trolley platform. If they cannot do it themselves, they are not ready to ride yet.

The last rule is worth underscoring. If an adult places a young child in a tree, it is much harder for the child to assess the risks of being up high. If the child has successfully climbed the tree on her own, then one can feel confident that she understands the height involved and the related risks.

Over time, children seek out more and more risks and learn to manage their own risk-taking. Dottie Hughes of the Huntington Beach Adventure Playground[49] near Los Angeles says, "Children search out and find risk. In this environment, they have more control over their own risk. On a traditional playground, where equipment is made in a certain way, you get kids climbing outside of the tube slide, climbing on the roof."[50]

Dottie Hughes also reports that there is a definite progression in how children approach what they perceive as risky experiences. At the beginning of the summer, the children typically wander around looking. They don't participate in some of the "scarier" play, such as rock climbing or the mud-pit zip line. Then, one or two boys will start to rock climb, going up, coming down, going up a bit farther, coming down—again and again until they reach the top. Or a child might climb part way up the rope and then quickly drop to the ground, look around as if saying to himself, "What have I done?" And then he'll try again.

> A child who is determined to climb to the top of a structure will practice over and over, carefully gauging her position and stretching further until she does it.

When playing freely among themselves, children discover their own levels of ability, practicing again and again the balancing, orienting, hand-grip strength, jumping, and other skills needed for active play. Emotional elements of fear, surprise, joy in mastery, and shared experiences contribute greatly to the experience.

A child who is determined to climb to the top of a structure will practice over and over, carefully gauging her position and stretching further until she does it. The girl who wants to build a playhouse will listen carefully

while the playworker demonstrates tool safety, then hammer away until her nails are straight and sure. Children are remarkably capable when given a chance to develop their skills.

The Parks District of Franklin Park, Illinois, for example, decided to increase the free play activities in its summer camp and other programs after a week-long training with London-based playworker Penny Wilson.[51] Playworkers work in adventure playgrounds, on schoolyards, in parks, and other settings where they help create playful environments and support play for children of all ages.

During Penny's training of the Franklin Park staff, a group of four-year-olds were invited to spend an afternoon in free play while the course participants observed them. The play included dress-ups, mud play, and play with loose parts, as well as hammering nails into a thick board. The staff, many of whom were not used to working with such young children, were astonished at how competent the children were and remarked on it during the review of the session. This was especially evident in their use of hammer and nails.[52] Joe Modrich, director of Parks and Recreation for Franklin Park, reports: "Children handle hammers and nails at their own comfort level. If adults are not hovering nearby, the children do what they can do."[53]

This observation brings to mind the oft-cited quote by Lev Vygotsky (1896-1934), the Russian educator and psychologist who was a strong proponent of play. "In play," he noted, "a child is always above his average age, above his daily behavior; in play, it is as though he were a head taller than himself."[54]

Children grow in confronting risk

Play which allows children to use their full abilities almost always incorporates some risk, whether it is physical, social, or intellectual. Risk is generally thought of only in physical terms, but it should be understood as a vital part of every aspect of development, not just the physical. Taking a chance that another child will accept you as a playmate or that you can resolve a conflict without adult intervention is a social risk.

When playing physically, children love to interact with the elements of earth, water, air, and fire (especially with the usually forbidden fire). According to English play theorist Bob Hughes, such play recalls how human beings developed over millennia. Hughes, who is an experienced playworker as well as an author and researcher, calls this type of play "recapitulative play." He describes it as those play routines that remind us of ancient cultures, such as using paints, masks, and body decorations to change identity; building caves and dens; and using weapons. He sees such play as a vital part of human evolution.[55]

Bob Hughes describes a close connection between recapitulative play and another play type—deep play. Deep play allows the child to encounter the things he or she most fears. It can seem very scary to the adult watching, for it is play generally full of risk. But Hughes describes how children approach such play with surprising caution and rarely experience injuries. He says children move through several levels of deep play.

Deep Play represents a very real journey on the part of every child who engages in it. Whether that journey includes standing up against a bully, climbing to a challenging height, swinging perilously close to solid objects, confronting a phobia… In a sense Deep Play should also be described in graduations: Deep Play 1, Deep Play 2, 3 and 4, and so on, because it is not the same experience over and over again. Deep Play 1, the child's first experience of Deep Play, is the most challenging and can for the first few times be equated with leaping over a metaphorical cliff. Although the risks are still there during later engagement… by then most children will have begun to accumulate skills to countermand these fears.

In my experience, it is very rare that children actually injure themselves when they engage in this play type. They extend their limits gradually and are only looking to experience a representation rather than the reality of death or damage. When they do, it normally means they have either been pushed by someone, or have pushed themselves significantly beyond their abilities. This possibility and its potential consequences should act as a serious reminder of the impact of peer pressure (or even playworker pressure), or the development of a culture between children in which they move past risk and engage in foolhardy or potentially suicidal activity of the serial thrill-seeker.[56]

In all, Hughes describes 16 types of play,[57] although he says the categories are fluid and most play contains several types merged together. He stresses the importance of children being given a chance to engage in all types of play. He feels this is especially important regarding deep play, which has a close relationship to thrill-seeking. This gives it a potentially addictive quality, which is normally balanced by children's interest in other play types, such as socio-dramatic play.

It is a challenge for adults to provide children with play opportunities that include the full range of play types. It is especially challenging when the children's play awakens fears in the adults. Are the fears reasonable or the remainders of one's own unresolved issues?

Stephen J. Smith, a professor of education at Simon Fraser University in British Columbia, has written a book entitled *Risk and Our Pedagogical Relation to Children*. He discusses risk in play from a parent's perspective and speaks of the constant sensitivity required to achieve that balance of risk and safety. He remarks that parents can be most helpful "if we know when our help is needed and when it is not." He says it is not easy but it is necessary to let go of "our apprehensions, our fears, and our unfounded sense of danger."[58]

Letting go of fears becomes easier when they are replaced with observations of children's ability to risk-assess. Watching how children approach playground equipment is one way to observe their risk-assessment. They may begin with great enthusiasm, then grow more cautious as they sense the risks involved, and then persist until they have mastered the equipment. This is most easily seen if they have a chance to return to the same playground a number of times.

By providing opportunities for play that carries some risk with it and levels of oversight appropriate to children's age and abilities, caring adults can help children develop their risk-assessment skills, just as they help children develop a host of other essential capacities.

Bringing risk into playgrounds

Some parks departments are recognizing children's need for risk. For example, one occasionally now sees zip lines in a public playground or equipment associated with risk. This is a change from the attitude that has dominated the thinking about playgrounds for the past half century or more. Susan Solomon, in her book *American Playgrounds: Revitalizing Community Space*, notes that "safety for its own sake" began to take over in the U.S. with increasing regulation in part because of lawsuits and a fear of them. Playground safety regulations were often divorced from actual data on accidents and injuries. They often did not relate to whether the equipment or the activity in question had ever contributed to any serious injuries.[59]

Susan Solomon also describes a visit in 1965 to U.S. playgrounds by Marjory Gill Allen, better known as Lady Allen of Hurtwood,[60] the passionate founder of adventure playgrounds in the U.K. Lady Allen was a British landscape architect who was very interested in children's play spaces. Just after World War II she traveled to Emdrup in Denmark to visit a "junk playground" that was created during the war. It was inspired by the work of Carl Theodor Sørensen, who had designed playgrounds before the war but now saw that children were not playing on them. They preferred playing amidst the rubble of bombed out buildings. The playground at Emdrup was full of "loose parts"—open-ended materials that could be played with in a myriad of ways.

Lady Allen visited the playground at Emdrup and later said, "I was completely swept off my feet by my first visit to Emdrup playground. In a flash of understanding I realized that I was looking at something quite new and full of possibilities. There was a wealth of waste material on it and no man-made fixtures. The children could dig, build houses, experiment with sand, water or fire and play games of adventure and make believe."[61]

She returned to London and worked hard to establish adventure playgrounds, as she called these somewhat quirky and messy play sites.

When Lady Allen traveled to the U.S in 1965 she observed the playgrounds that were then being built and was shocked by their sterility and barren landscapes. She felt they were constructed with low maintenance uppermost in the minds of designers and commented that they were "an administrator's heaven and a child's hell... [Americans] seem to be terrified of risk—they are dogged by fear of insurance claims resulting from accidents in public playgrounds. I've never seen anything like it!"[62]

The history of playgrounds in the U.S. is a complex one. A brief but very informative picture is available in an article by Amanda Erikson entitled "The Politics of Playgrounds, a History."[63] For a much fuller history see Susan Solomon's book, *American Playgrounds*.[64]

Solomon's web site includes ten tips for designing a good playground and says this about "acceptable risk":

> Playgrounds need a basic level of safety. It's hard to talk about (who, after all, ever wants to see a kid hurt?) but playgrounds also need a certain level of acceptable risk. Overly safe playgrounds inhibit kids from becoming mature adults.[65]

Joe Frost has made a lifelong study of play and playgrounds.[66] He has helped research playground equipment and has given expert testimony in court cases involving playground injuries. "Perhaps the most significant missed opportunity for making American playgrounds safer and developmentally appropriate," he says, "was failure to promote and adopt principles and practices of adventure playgrounds."[67] Adventure playgrounds failed to gain popularity in the United States, he adds, because of "adults' perceptions of their unsightly appearance, unsubstantiated safety concerns, lack of understanding of the value of spontaneous, creative play and games, and lack of funding."[68]

In the U.K. and other parts of Europe, adventure playgrounds have found a more welcoming home. Fortunately we hear of renewed interest in them in the U.S. A short list of existing ones can be found in the Resources section. We discuss lessons learned from adventure playgrounds, in terms of providing play opportunities for healthy risk-taking, in more detail in Chapter Three.

CHAPTER THREE

Lessons about Risk
from Adventure Playgrounds

Better a broken bone than a broken spirit.[69]

— Lady Allen of Hurtwood

Adventure playgrounds provide a unique lens for studying adventurous play and risk. They are staffed with playworkers, and data is kept on accidents. In contrast, adventuresome play in the woods and fields—or in the storm sewers of New York, a popular activity in previous decades—goes largely unobserved by adults. Such play provides rich opportunities for children, but very few have a chance to experience it any longer.

Joe Frost notes that even children in rural areas no longer have access to the same rich environments for play as in the past:

Until recently, children in the country enjoyed the advantages of adventure playgrounds in their everyday play lives. Traffic was rarely a danger. There were trees to climb, dense bushes to create hiding places and forts, woods for exploring, fires to be made for cooking, animals to be chased, and tree houses to be built. Raw materials for building dens and forts were everywhere. Rivers, creeks, and ponds were available for swimming and fishing, and adults working in the fields and hunting in the woods were frequently available for advice and models. But all this changed as country kids joined their city peers in the mass exodus to indoor cyber worlds.[70]

In a 2007 interview, Frost elaborates on what constitutes good play:

"When I was a boy in rural Arkansas recess meant roaming through hills, woods, fields and creeks around the school, and we went out to play multiple times a day. Adult supervision was minimal, kids developed terrific motor skills and there were few or no serious injuries. We've complicated something so essentially innocent and straightforward—kids just need a safe setting where they can become strong and resilient and develop into thinkers, builders, creators and explorers."[71]

Children still need to be allowed to play freely on their own and with their peers. Many of today's adults would have been appalled if their parents tagged along while they played in woods, fields, and city alleys once they reached school age. One of the best ways the Alliance for Childhood has found to compensate for the loss of opportunity for free play, as Joe Frost describes it above, is through the creation of adventure playgrounds, staffed with well-educated playworkers who provide oversight and support but who are trained not to dictate, direct, or dominate children's play.

If children are no longer free to go outdoors with friends and create their own worlds, then society needs to offer them the best alternatives possible, and adventure playgrounds with well-trained staff fill that need.

While the adventure playground movement began in England in the 1940's just after World War II, in the U.S. the founding of adventure playgrounds did not take hold until the 1970's. An American Adventure Playground Association was formed in 1976, and by 1977 the AAPA had identified 16 sites in the United States. Play advocates say there were others scattered around the country that were not included in that count. Slowly, however, these play sites began to close down. Today we know of only four public adventure playgrounds in the U.S. Three are in California and one in the state of Washington. Their locations can be found in the Resources list in this document.

Why did so many adventure playgrounds close and so few open to take their place? Joe Frost, who has watched the rise and fall of the adventure play movement in this country, sums up the problems in this way:

> The life span for most American adventure playgrounds was short, due to concerns about junky appearance, expansion of safety regulations, fear of injury and liability, shortage of funding and play leaders, and lack of support from community leaders. Despite their strong reputation among developers, child users, and involved parents, most disappeared but a few model examples remain.[72]

Let's take a closer look at adults' concerns, and the benefits these play spaces provide.

1. Unsubstantiated safety concerns and fear of litigation. As we mention later in this publication, we can find no evidence that adventure playgrounds are more dangerous than conventional ones or that they lead to a significant number of lawsuits. An important point is that insurance companies do not charge parks departments extra for having an adventure playground. An adventure playground is not viewed as more dangerous than a community swimming pool, for example, and the same liability levels of coverage apply.

2. The cost of staffing the playgrounds seems prohibitive. It is true that adventure playgrounds are generally staffed with playworkers, and this is a cost not usually associated with playgrounds. Whether a community finds this investment worthwhile has much to do with its understanding of play and the value of risk. Most communities invest in swimming pools and lifeguards, for they recognize the value of swimming. Why not also invest in adventure playgrounds and playworkers? It can be argued that they provide equal value to the children and the community.

3. Adults find the appearance of adventure playgrounds unsightly. When I asked Patty Donald of the Berkeley Adventure Playground why more communities did not establish these great play spaces for children, she immediately answered, "NIMBY"—not in my backyard.[73] They do look messy, and I recall looking at a photo of an adventure playground in Switzerland[74] and being astonished that that neat and tidy country was home to such a playground. It looked incredibly ramshackle. When I visited it a few years later, I was delighted to find it looked just as it had in the photo—messy but highly creative and quirky. High-rise apartment buildings overlooked the site, but there was also an adjoining park dotted with modern sculptures.

It is easy to see the messiness of an adventure playground. What is harder to see are the stories, dramas, and re-enactments that are taking place in those child-built structures. Throughout the adventure playground, make-believe play is taking place along with construction play, mastery play, rough and tumble play, and other forms that play experts find essential for a child's overall healthy development.[75]

Seventy years of childhood adventures

The original adventure playground, as noted earlier, arose in Denmark during World War II. The idea was first proposed by Carl Theodor Sørensen, a Danish landscape architect. Its origins have been ably recounted by Joe Frost:

> [Sørensen's] proposal was tested during the German occupation in 1943 when he created a "junk playground" in Emdrup, a housing estate on the outskirts of Copenhagen. Long before World War II, indeed over centuries, children played in construction sites, garbage dumps, junk yards and wild places, found and borrowed their own tools, built their own dens, forts and houses, and played their own creative games—all without the unwavering supervision of adults. Sørensen's dream included trained play leaders. John Bertelsen was the first play leader at Emdrup, enabled by architect and former seaman Dan Fink. True to Bertelson's views, the central idea of Sørensen's junk playgrounds was to make play and playgrounds the imagination of the child—not the imagination of the architect or builder. Children themselves, with assistance from playleaders, later called playworkers in the UK, would create playgrounds for themselves and choose their own play objects and forms of play. To modern eyes, attuned to fixed, immutable playgrounds, dominating cyber play and endless prescribed regulations, all this reverberates as romantic, archaic, and even threatening.[76]

Several years ago, a National Public Radio reporter described a similar scene at the Berkeley Adventure Playground, which was created in 1979 and is still open:[77]

> Scattered around the one-acre lot are at least 15 wooden forts of varying size—some two stories high, others with only two walls. They're all covered in paint, and many bear the names of the children who had a hand in their creation: Sophie, Bobby, Roger, Morita. There are also piles of scrap wood, old boats, fishing-net, tires, you name it.[78]

The Land, Wales

Photo: Erin Davis

The oldest existing adventure playground in the U.S. is in Huntington Beach near Los Angeles. Joe Frost describes it this way:

> The oldest true adventure playground in the United States opened in 1974 in Huntington Beach and was moved to a new site in 1981. True to tradition, the playground features such "to kill for" adventures as a 16 feet mud slide, rafting pond with rope bridge, tire swing, tools and scrap (donated material) for building and outdoor showers and changing rooms. Six "counselors" oversee these and other activities such as overnight campouts. The playground was named recreation program of the year by the California Parks and Recreation Society.[79]

What stands out at adventure play sites are activities not seen on typical playgrounds: playing on zip lines; using hammers, nails, saws, and other tools; climbing very high on play structures, slides, and tree houses; tending fires with adults, rolling down hills in barrels, and much more.

Halcyon Reese-Learned provided these descriptions of adventure playgrounds in her report to the Alliance for Childhood:

> The California programs regularly have 150 children in the morning and the same number in the afternoon. At the Houston program, 60 children were enrolled in an afterschool program for the entire school year.

The activities that the children in Adventure Play programs participate in may include those of more traditional programs, such as group games, singing, running and climbing, but many more that are decidedly different. Instead of adult-led crafts, the participating children conduct open-ended experimentation and construction with raw and recycled materials, using tools such as hammers, saws, hand-held drills, and shovels. Instead of climbing on commercially-made equipment, they construct and grasp, under trained adult supervision, zip lines, and they slide in mud pits and wade in a shallow pond with child-made rafts. Instead of digging with plastic trowels in small sandboxes, they dig with real shovels in large and deep sand pits.

Because the Adventure Play experience for children is usually conducted on a site with a surrounding fence and is relatively secure from vandalism, another distinguishing feature is that the children's constructions can stay for long periods of time, so that they can add on to them day after subsequent day. The fort with a tarp over tree branches, the "speed chair" made from a donated office chair spruced up with handles, the pool table with pockets made from mosquito netting are there to greet the children who eagerly return to their creations each day, refining with renewed experimentation, until they, not the adult (unless there is a health or safety concern), decide it is time to move on to something else.[80]

An essential part of adventure playgrounds is the abundance of "loose parts" or basic materials that children can use in multiple ways. They are described by Penny Wilson in *The Playwork Primer*:

[L]oose parts refers to anything that can be moved around, carried, rolled, lifted, piled on top of one another, or combined to create interesting and novel structures and experiences. Loose parts include wood, containers, shapes, toys, animals, plants, and so on.... Loose parts liberate the imagination and creativity of the playing children and allow them to master the world around them in ever-changing ways and communicate more effectively through their playing.[81]

Children love to build, and adventure playgrounds give them a chance to do so with hammer, nails, and lumber, often donated by local contractors. When I visited the adventure playground Holzwurm outside Zurich, Switzerland several years ago,[82] I saw structures three stories high built by school-age children. There were also large tree houses. One was especially high in a tree, built by a 16-year-old as his farewell gift to the playground. He'd been coming there since he was six.

> *Adventure playgrounds not only challenge children's physical skills, they also provide opportunities for rich social interaction.*

The children's play houses were furnished with cast-off furniture and even an old piano. Such structures appear flimsy, as if the first strong wind would blow them over, but the children test their structures as they build and also use so many nails in building them that the houses don't fall down. Eventually adults cut them down with a chain saw to make room for more buildings.

It is not unusual to see bonfires at adventure playgrounds, tended by the playworkers. At Glamis Adventure Playground in the East End of London, for instance, playworkers tend the fire and prepare an afternoon tea time snack for the children. When I visited on a chilly January day, the children began arriving after school when it was already getting dark and stayed until 7 or 8 p.m., when the playground closed. The bonfire provided welcome warmth, and the hot snack did too.

Another description of a European adventure playground comes from Alex Gilliam, founder and director of Public Workshop,[83] a consulting group that brings the voices of youth into the design of schools and communities. Gilliam helped dozens of teens, young designers, and families design and build a pop-up adventure playground in downtown Philadelphia last fall,[84] after visiting an adventure playground in Berlin called Kolle 37. Of the Berlin playground, he reports:

Even if you just spend fifteen minutes watching closely, you will witness children testing their creation for sturdiness, stability and load. Testing in this fashion is how they learn. Sometimes their solutions for an overly flexible bridge or a sagging railing are not the most aesthetically pleasing or efficient material wise, but they will keep adding, shifting or changing until it feels safe...

Kolle 37 is a particularly amazing playground. Between the diversity of activities on the site (a stage, a kitchen, an art studio, a forge, a fire pit, a teen-run bike shop, a waffle stand, a rock climbing wall, farm animals, and a preschool playground) and the respect (and support) that they give children, it's a truly remarkable place that really draws into question how we treat children in this country. Not only are they giving children a multiplicity of opportunities to explore and create but some of their simplest rules implicitly teach such important things as teamwork, and citizenship. Most importantly, nothing is more empowering or educational than the act of 'doing' and I can't begin to tell you how many students I encounter in my work who have been taught to be passive—to not challenge or wonder.[85]

Adventure playgrounds not only challenge children's physical skills, they also provide opportunities for rich social interaction. This is especially true for children who come regularly to a play site and have many opportunities to play together. At adventure playgrounds that feature building, for instance, the children continually negotiate as they create the structures they need for play. Their conversations are rarely captured. But Lia Sutton, who visited a number of adventure playgrounds as part of her senior project at Hampshire College, included this conversation on her website, "Adventure Playgrounds: A children's world in the city:"[86]

Beth calls out to Sam, "Come help me and my friend Matt build something." "Sure," says Sam...

"We could build a pirate ship," says Beth. "...Or a house and then we could build furniture," says Matt. "We should build a tree house and a ladder to climb into it," says Sam. "...Or a post office," says Matt.

"Yeah! And then everyone could have mailboxes so their mail wouldn't get lost," says Beth. "Yeah, and

all the houses could have numbers so they know where to deliver the mail," says Matt. "That would be so cool!" says Beth. "Let's do it."

"Okay, so what do we need?" wonders Sam. "Hmmm, okay Matt, you get three hammers and some nails... I'll get the wood," says Beth. "Where should we build it?" says Sam. "In the center of all the forts and houses in the playground!" says Beth. "Yeah, how 'bout next to Jaime and Molly's house?" asks Matt.

"Awesome," says Beth.

One can imagine this play continuing over long periods of time if the children are given a chance. Play weaves children together into a rich social body. Such play is beautifully described in the 1991 children's book, *Roxaboxen*,[87] by Alice McLerran. It describes the play of a group of neighborhood children who created their own village on a scruffy bit of land up the hill from their homes. They developed Roxaboxen over years. McLerran's mother was one of the children, and decades later McLerran interviewed those who played in Roxaboxen as children and collected their rich memories of play into another book called *The Legacy of Roxaboxen*.[88] Many in the group remained connected throughout life. McLerran comments:

I should add that not only my mother but every Roxaboxenite I came to know was in adult life an interesting, articulate, and good person. I can't help thinking that what they created together on that hill—the shared and independent play, the comfortable silences and the long conversations—had something to do with it. They could learn leadership and cooperation; they could develop initiative and independence and imagination. The ever-deepening bonds of friendship taught them much about loyalty and generosity of spirit.

I wish every child could have a Roxaboxen.[89]

We wish it too. But the reality is that today's children are rarely given the space or the time for such open-ended, unsupervised play. A major obstacle is adult fear, which results in limited freedom for children's play. Adventure playgrounds, staffed with playworkers, are a way of compensating for what is lost. The playworkers provide a presence that is reassuring to parents. But they hold back from intervening in the children's play, which is a boon for the children. They step in only if it seems clear that a child is likely to hurt himself or another child. Penny Wilson describes the cape of invisibility that playworkers wear. They give children a sense of freedom such as the Roxaboxen children had, but at the same time the cape can be taken off when the playworker needs to intervene.

It's our hope that communities will begin developing adventure playgrounds to meet the needs of children for adventurous, child-directed play with open-ended materials. Obstacles that are frequently suggested are accident rates and lawsuits, but as we discuss in Chapters Four and Five, accident rates are no greater than on other playgrounds and are probably less, and lawsuits have been very rare over a 30-year period. It is true that adventure playgrounds need staffing, which is an expense, but the gains in children's overall health and development more than compensate for the cost. A combination of public and private funding should be able to cover these costs. The final objection mentioned is that they are unattractive. It is true that they often look like a shanty town, but a charming child-built one. In the end this seems like a minor problem compared to a generation growing up without a wide range of play opportunities.

The playworker's office at The Land, Wales

Photo: Erin Davis

CHAPTER FOUR

Injury Rates Relatively Low for Adventure Playgrounds

> *The Royal Society for the Prevention of Accidents (U.K.) confirms that the accident record of adventure playgrounds is far better than that of other forms of [play] provision.*[90]
>
> — The Royal Society for the Prevention of Accidents

Most people look at adventure playgrounds, see that they have risky play activities such as sawing and hammering, and playing on zip lines, and then assume the accident rate is much higher than on conventional playgrounds. Yet data from U.S. and U.K. adventure playgrounds support a different view. While more thorough data would be helpful, the information that does exist indicates that, taking comparable numbers of children into account, there are the same or fewer emergency-room type injuries per child on adventure play sites than on conventional playgrounds. The low accident rates are very likely related to the children's own growing physical prowess. As children become more aware of their physical skills and limitations, they grow more proficient at assessing risks for themselves.

In 2001 the highly respected National Children's Bureau in the U.K. was asked to "examine evidence surrounding accidents, risk, perception of risk and risk management at adventure playgrounds" in three of London's boroughs. There were a total of 26 adventure playgrounds in the three boroughs, and half of them participated in the study. The results of the study are available on the web site of London Play. "Accidents, particularly serious accidents," the study found, "were rare at the adventure playgrounds."[91]

A Canadian study commissioned in 1976 reviewed safety on adventure and traditional playgrounds. The authors noted that while strict comparisons were not possible because of a lack of systematic record-keeping, the qualitative accounts from particular adventure playgrounds reported that the accidents were low in frequency and severity. One such account reads:

> From July 14 to August 27, 1971, 1512 children participated in the program at Ottawa's Wellington Adventure Playground. The incidence of accidents at this playground was lower than in the traditional playground. Children seem to be more careful when they know that they are handling tools that are potentially dangerous.[92]

This last comment is especially important. Observers of children's play often comment that when children are given genuine risk they "rise to it" and exercise appropriate judgment. In other words, they assess risk and make good choices.

According to a fact sheet produced by the Centers for Disease Control and Prevention,[93] each year over 200,000 children age 14 and younger go to emergency rooms for treatment of accidents on playgrounds. Tragically, about 15 children die each year as a result of playground injuries.

Joe Frost has given expert testimony in about 200 lawsuits brought in conjunction with injuries on traditional playgrounds. He reports that the problems are generally from "poor design and improper maintenance."[94] He also notes that he has visited adventure play sites in

Europe and the U.S. many times, but he has never spoken with anyone knowledgeable about adventure playgrounds who thought the sites were more dangerous than traditional playgrounds.

While reports indicate that adventure playgrounds have a surprisingly low rate of injuries, some accidents do occur. The Houston adventure play programs existed in various forms (drop-in, afterschool, and in public parks) over a period of fifteen years, from 1980 to 1995. The Mountain Park project, a parent-child drop-in

© photosearch.com

program in operation there for four years, recorded minor injuries. At the afterschool programs on public school campuses, minor incidents such as tripping, abrasions, and insect bites were fairly common, but the program recorded in 15 years only four instances of children needing emergency room visits. The injuries requiring emergency treatment involved children stepping on nails, a cut on the head, and a broken arm.[95]

The California adventure playgrounds report similar low injury rates. Berkeley's year-round drop-in program, in operation since 1979, has not recorded injuries systematically. The program director, Patty Donald, reports that there have been few emergency-room injuries, but some injuries have occurred in the playground's 30-plus years. "A child hit his finger with a hammer, children have gotten bruises, punctures, a couple of broken arms, and one child lost two teeth from the zip line."[96] The latter happened only once. In her 2005 review of American playgrounds, Susan Solomon wrote about the Berkeley program:

> Berkeley's adventure playground has not been an exception when it comes to a sound safety record. Berkeley officials have long maintained that the adventure playground gives the illusion of danger while offering a safe space for personal development.[97]

The mayor of Berkeley, Tom Bates, reported in 2009 that he relished his visits to the adventure playground with his then seven-year-old grandson. When asked about the injury rates, he responded that he had never heard of any serious injuries there and, in fact, had never once received a complaint from a parent about the program. This was, he noted, in stark contrast with the number of complaints and lawsuits related to injuries from falls on the sidewalks.[98]

When many adults think of adventurous play they become fearful and shy away from it. Yet they enroll their children in organized sports or transport them in cars, even though there are many injuries associated with these valued activities. For example, the Safe Kids Campaign and the American Academy of Pediatrics report that "More than 775,000 children ages 14 and under are treated in hospital emergency rooms for sports-related injuries each year."[99] Regarding car accidents, over 1,600 children under 15 years of age die each year.[100]

We realize that there are far fewer children playing at adventure playgrounds than are participating in sports, being driven in cars, or playing on conventional playgrounds, making comparisons difficult. But the high value of adventurous play and the need for children to develop skills for risk assessment should outweigh the small incidence of injuries. When people value an activity enough they seek to minimize hazards and avoid serious injuries—but they do accept the risks that remain, as with organized sports or car travel, as noted above.

It's time to develop the same attitude toward adventurous play with these guidelines in mind: Understand the importance of such play for children's overall development; seek to avoid serious injuries; and accept the risks of relatively minor injury that remain. As children develop their physical skills and capacity for risk assessment, it may well turn out that adventurous play with moderate levels of risk is one of the safest and healthiest opportunities they can engage in.

Managing Risk

> *Children need and want to take risks when they play. Play provision aims to respond to these needs and wishes by offering children stimulating, challenging environments for exploring and developing their abilities. In doing this, play provision aims to manage the level of risk so that children are not exposed to unacceptable risks of death or serious injury.*[101]
>
> — The Play Safety Forum of England

Rather than avoiding risk on playgrounds, many play programs now talk about managing it or even going a step further and doing risk-benefit assessment, which includes evaluating benefits as well as risks. The insurance industry practices risk management, which can be useful in evaluating risk on adventure playgrounds. Risk management is the "process of identifying conditions that can cause injury or loss of assets, then devising strategies to eliminate or control those conditions."[102]

In the insurance industry, risk management is frequently described as having three critical parts:

1. *Develop techniques to reduce hazards or other potential exposure to loss.*

2. *Provide systematic risk analysis.*

3. *Procure and administer insurance.*

What does risk management look like when applied to adventure play programs?

Reducing hazards

The first step in risk management is to identify *hazards* on the playground. A hazard, as contrasted with a risk, has been defined as something that the child cannot be expected to see and therefore cannot avoid. A stone or a tree root sticking out of the ground in the middle of an open field can be considered a hazard, because the child expects to be able to run freely through that space and is not looking for obstacles on which she might trip. A bolt or screw protruding from a piece of playground equipment that could poke a child is a hazard, as is a gap where a string from a child's jacket could get caught and choke him.

Checking a playground regularly for hazards is a long-established practice in supervised play areas and adventure playgrounds are no exception. Indeed, the fact that playworkers are on hand daily at adventure playgrounds means the play spaces receive more frequent safety inspections by staff than do conventional playgrounds. This may contribute to their low levels of serious injuries.

Risk analysis

In risk analysis, activities that are considered to be of significant risk are reviewed for age- and developmental-appropriateness. For instance, one common activity on adventure play sites is fort or clubhouse building. It is always an immensely popular activity for the children, both girls and boys.

For younger children dragging tree branches together and draping canvas tarps over them constitutes a suitable shelter for play. Older children expand their building techniques with the use of tools. The risks involved in constructing with hammers and nails are dealt with through adult oversight as well as proper equipment. Some adventure playgrounds provide specific training in the use of tools. Others have found that is not necessary, although adult oversight is provided. A common safety measure is that children who want to use hammer and nails must first collect discarded nails found on the ground. The playgrounds are often strict about the children wearing sturdy shoes to avoid injury, rather than flip-flops or open sandals.

Risk analysis can be applied to any play activity, especially to new ones that are being introduced. Suzanna Law, a playworker in England and co-director of Pop-Up Adventure Play,[103] used the process for a new activity. She explained how she risk-assessed when she wanted to introduce a small fire pit to do cooking with the children at an adventure play program near Manchester. As potential risks, she mentioned: risk of burns from flames, ash or hot objects; smoke inhalation; sloping terrain; risk of fire spilling out of the container and causing burns or other small fires; and risk of burns from hot food.

The "control measures" she proposed were: supervision and full briefing before activity; having a plunge bucket and extra bottles of water and a water supply nearby; and evening out the terrain with rocks/bricks.[104] Such assessments bring heightened consciousness about identifying and managing risk and also calm fears about adventure play. There is always the danger, however, that the assessment will become overly bureaucratic, and the adventure play will lose some of the spontaneity that is such an important part of it.

Risk-benefit analysis goes a step further than risk management. It recognizes that many activities carry benefits at the same time that they carry risks. Both risks and benefits need to be examined and weighed against each other. Thus, although data show that many children are injured participating in sports, adults recognize the benefits of the activity and accept the risks that go with it. Consciously or unconsciously adults engage in risk-benefit analysis and weigh the risks with the benefits. The steps in risk-benefit analysis, along with examples, are given in an excellent report published by Play England, a prominent play organization that has published many valuable documents. Its document called *Managing Risk in Play Provision*[105] contains two chapters (six and seven) that are especially devoted to risk-benefit analysis.

A further development in risk analysis is a process called "dynamic risk assessment," which is often defined as risk assessment in a rapidly changing environment. While traditional risk assessment may suffice on conventional playgrounds, adventure playgrounds are finding they need a more dynamic model. It is not enough to check fixed equipment at the beginning of the day. The staff needs to assess new situations as they arise. Playworkers are skilled in observing children and the environment, and they continually assess whether the child is able to handle the amount of risk he or she is undertaking. They also share their observations with one another during regular review sessions, ideally held at the end of each day.

Insurance

The threat of lawsuits and liability is often the first concern that municipalities and other sponsoring groups raise when faced with the prospect of creating an adventure play program in their communities. The explosive growth of lawsuits in the United States has resulted in city councils and parks and recreation departments being wary about sponsoring children's programs with which they are unfamiliar.

The litigious atmosphere in the United States is much stronger than in Europe and Japan, where adventure playgrounds continue to thrive. Given the American tendency to sue, we might expect a fairly large number of lawsuits in regard to adventure playgrounds in the U.S. However, the experience of adventure playgrounds in the U.S. regarding insurance, lawsuits, and liability issues has, like their safety record, been quite positive.

When the Huntington Beach adventure play program first began operating in the 1970s, the staff persuaded the insurance company to monitor its safety record and also the safety records of conventional playgrounds in the city. After three summers, the insurance company determined that the adventure playground's safety record closely matched that of the traditional playgrounds. No additional insurance premiums were thus required.[106] Over the years there has been one lawsuit at this site, according to Dottie Hughes, the playground's longtime manager. A child fractured his ankle on the water slide and the parent sued. The city settled out of court with the parent and there have been no other lawsuits, according to Hughes.[107]

Irvine Adventure Play has had no lawsuits,[108] and Bill Sellin, the supervisor of this adventure playground in Irvine, CA, reports that "the Risk Management Department is very comfortable with the adventure play program."[109]

The Houston adventure play programs were either on school campuses, in which case the children were covered by their school insurance with no additional premiums, or at a public park, where no additional insurance was deemed necessary by the parks and recreation department. The umbrella association for Houston's adventure playgrounds, however, also carried general liability insurance.

The U.S. Adventure Playground Report mentioned previously, that surveyed 16 U.S. adventure playgrounds during the 1970s, also reviewed what arrangements existed for insurance in programs operated by local government agencies. It found that all of them were operating under the liability insurance policies that were already in place and that no additional insurance premiums were specifically needed for the adventure play sites.[110]

All in all, the record of adventure playgrounds indicates that they can be operated at least as safely as traditional playgrounds and that lawsuits have not been a major problem for the adventure playgrounds. Further, they impose no special insurance concerns or costs. All of this is good news for municipalities, schools, and others interested in reviving children's play by creating new adventure playgrounds. And it's wonderful news for children, who will benefit from experiencing more adventure in their play.

© photosearch.com

CHAPTER SIX

Next Steps

> *Children extend their abilities through risky play and learn to master challenging environments. They generally know how far they can go without actually hurting themselves.*[111]
>
> — Alliance for Childhood, *Crisis in the Kindergarten*

For this publication, we have highlighted how risk is handled at adventure playgrounds to both inform and inspire. But such playgrounds provide just one example of the ways adults can support children's spirit of adventure and help them develop their capacity for risk assessment. There are many other places that also focus on risk in interesting ways, such as the City Museum in St. Louis, which is famous for its adventurous play opportunities.[112] KaBOOM!'s web site also features photos of "dangerous playgrounds"[113] and interesting playgrounds made of junk.[114] Families can also add elements of adventure in their own play areas in age-appropriate ways, and one increasingly sees tree houses and child-constructed forts in private yards.

It is time to grow beyond being pro-risk or anti-risk and instead develop a nuanced understanding of risk that takes a child's full development into account. To do so, one can turn to experts, and among the world's experts on play and risk are the children themselves.

Listening to children

Children have both passion and insights about play and risk. In addition, their right to be consulted on matters that concern their lives is articulated in the U.N.'s Convention on the Rights of the Child (CRC). The fact that the U.S. has not yet ratified the CRC does not mean that we should ignore its contents, which are vital to the health and well-being of all children.

Article 12 of the CRC assures a child the right "to express his or her opinion freely and to have that opinion taken into account in any matter or procedure affecting the child." Many countries now work hard to include the voices of children when setting policies that affect children. This does not mean that children have authority over adults but that their views are sought after and respected. Weight is given to their opinions "in accordance with the age and maturity of the child."[115]

Sometimes the views of children and especially teen-agers are hard for adults to hear, but they are worthwhile, nonetheless. An example is the view of Hannan, a teen-ager in England who speaks bluntly:

> To be honest, adults can be very stupid at times. They ban everything for health and safety reasons. If they're going to ban very simple stuff like this [playing tag], they might as well lock all kids in empty rooms to keep them safe. Kids should be allowed to experiment and try things. Otherwise when they grow up they'll make very stupid mistakes from not getting enough experience at childhood.[116]

When David Hawkins and Karen Payne, founders of Wild-Zones, which encourages nature play for children and youth, wanted expert advice on the problems of risk deprivation, they turned to their experts—teenagers. The teens made these points:[117]

- Kids need to experience moderate risk in order to assess larger risks
- Risk-deprivation can lead to excess risk
- Risk-deprivation can lead to lack of courage and confidence
- Interesting and exciting physical activity is appealing to kids so they are more likely to participate — reduces obesity
- Risk-taking can develop trust and team-building
- It's life!

The research of Julie Nicholson and others at Mills College, in which 61 children from ages three to 17 were interviewed about play, also showed that children have very strong feelings on the subject of play deprivation and value active play. The researchers asked them, "If adults said that play wasn't important for children, what would you say to them?" Julie Nicholson reports:

All of the children expressed disagreement and several had strong non-verbal reactions to accompany their responses. Examples of the statements of disagreement include: "That's not kind to say" (4 year old girl); "It is [important]! I would like, yell in their face!" (5 year old girl); "[I would say] That they're wrong! [slapped her hand down on the table]" (10 year old girl); "I'd say that is not true at all, it's really stupid, and I think everybody needs to play" (8 year old boy); and one 10 year old boy yelled, "YOU'RE JUST PLAIN OUT WRONG!"

Other children responded with justifications for the importance of play explaining that play was important because it gives you "more energy" (6 year old girl) and play is "what kids get to do before they get old" (10 year old girl). One 10 year old girl encouraged adults to "think more" provoking them to "think about it. You know, like, if you didn't play when you were a kid, what would you be like now?" Finally, some children constructed hypotheses to try to explain why adults' reasoning was misguided, as exemplified by an 11 year old girl who responded as if speaking directly to the adults proclaiming play's lack of importance: "You probably didn't get enough play when you were a kid and that's what you think."[118]

Julie Nicholson's research also elicited an unexpected answer from the children. It doesn't directly address the question of risk, but it does counter the popular assumption that children want to stay inside with their screens, rather than actively playing outdoors. When the children were asked to describe a play experience they thought was really fun, they mentioned three main themes: playing with others, playing outdoors, and playing with toys. Only two mentioned digital play among their favorite play experiences.

When I mentioned this relative disinterest in screen play to Christine Chen, founder and president of the Association for Early Childhood Educators in Singapore, she said she received very similar responses from kindergarten children in Singapore when she asked them how they'd like to spend a free day. They strongly favored outdoor play over screen time.[119]

Listening to parents and professionals

The voices of parents, especially those who are working to overcome fear and allow reasonable risk, also enrich one's understanding of play and risk. For example, Liza Sullivan, a play advocate in the Chicago area, began to consciously address issues of risk when her twins were three. She writes:

"When my twins asked me if they could get hurt, I warned them that falling was a possibility, but that I trusted them to make decisions based on their own abilities and comfort levels. They did just that, without any injuries, and with growing self-confidence, pride, and ability to coach themselves through difficult personal challenges."[120]

Finally, there is much to be learned from programs that prepare children and teens for fairly risky activities, such as skateboarding, building with power tools, racing and jumping with horses, mastering circus activities, and parkour. Their approaches to risk and what they are learning about how children handle risk could significantly enhance the field of adventurous play. This is an area that needs research.

Steps to Take

The following steps can help parents and professionals become more comfortable with adventurous play and help them support it on a broad scale.

1. **Think about the degree of risk your child or group can handle** and then offer them opportunities within that range. Be watchful, but hold back as much as you can from interfering.

2. **Encourage play at home and in your neighborhood.** Organize play days in parks and other settings. Provide loose parts—open-ended materials such as boxes, tape and fabric, scrap objects, and appropriate building materials and tools. Play days with nature objects in natural settings are also very popular and helpful for reconnecting children with nature.[121]

3. **Form groups of children who regularly go out to play together**, preferably in natural settings. Consider it an adventure play club. Provide adult oversight as needed, but let the adults be as non-intrusive as possible so that the children can organize their own play.[122]

4. **Parents and professionals working with children can inform themselves about the importance of play and risk and become advocates for play.** For background, read informative books and view videos and web sites on this topic. See the Resources listed in this document for some basic materials. Sign up for play web sites that provide regular updates on play issues and activities.[123]

5. **Want to advocate on a bigger scale?** Build local coalitions for play that bring together recreation workers, educators, environmentalists, park and school officials, health professionals, play advocates, parents, and others. Together you can assess your community's strengths and weaknesses in regard to adventurous play and also work to improve the opportunities. Consider becoming recognized as a Playful City through KaBOOM![124]

6. **Encourage park departments to develop adventure playgrounds** with playworkers present. If year-round or summer-long programs are not possible at first, encourage a week-long adventure play camp during the summer. At the very least, encourage a series of play days in different seasons that introduce children to adventurous play. Include water play, mud play, fort building, and similar activities suitable to the season. Bring a similar message to organizations that sponsor summer camps and children's activities, such as YMCA and YWCA programs, Jewish Community Centers, Boys and Girls Clubs, nature centers, children's museums, and others.

7. **Organize talks, workshops, or film screenings** with discussion about the need for play and risk in children's lives. Such presentations can be offered by those who understand the research and theoretical underpinnings of risk and play, and those who offer such opportunities to children on a regular basis.

In conclusion

Risk is something children need to encounter all through childhood. They are capable of risk-assessment from a young age, and this vital ability develops through use. Offering children opportunities to master risk is something every adult can do—at home, and in child care centers, schools, and out-of-school programs. You can start slowly and watch your confidence in your own ability to risk-assess grow, along with the children's ability to assess and handle risk.

Endnotes

Introduction

1 Diane Ackerman, *Deep Play*, Random House/Vintage Books (New York: 1999), p. 7. Chapter one of the book, which contains this quote, is available on-line at http://www.nytimes.com/books/first/a/ackerman-play.html

2 A partial list of recent books, articles, and films about play can be found in the Resources list in this publication.

3 Maritta Hännikainen, Elly Singer, and Bert van Oers, "Promoting play for a better future," *European Early Childhood Education Research Journal*, Volume 21, Issue 2, (2013), p. 165.

4 *Play Matters: A study of best practices to inform local policy and process in support of children's play, KaBOOM!* (Washington, DC: no date given), p. 13. The publication describes a Harris poll of 1,677 parents regarding play, commissioned by KaBOOM!, and a study by Yale psychologists Dorothy and Jerome Singer of 2,400 parents worldwide. http://kaboom.org/docs/documents/pdf/playmatters/Play_Matters_Extended_Case_Studies.pdf
Similar findings appeared in a study of 830 mothers nationwide. See: Rhonda Clements, "An Investigation of the Status of Outdoor Play," *Contemporary Issues in Early Childhood*, Volume 5, Issue 1, (2004). At http://www.imaginationplayground.com/images/content/2/9/2960/An-investigation-Of-The-Status-Of-Outdoor-Play.pdf. (Web sites accessed July 14, 2013).

5 Sources include "Adventure Playgrounds: A History (part 2)" by Janet Petitpas and others of Museums Now, at http://museums-now.blogspot.com/2011/08/adventure-playgrounds-history-part-2-in.html; and Lia Sutton's on-line booklet, "Adventure Playgrounds: A children's world in the city" at http://adventureplaygrounds.hampshire.edu/history.html (both accessed June 22, 2013).

6 "Adventure Playgrounds," a video by the National Playing Fields Association; a Stanley Schofield Production on YouTube at http://www.youtube.com/watch?v=Uwj1wh5k5PY (accessed June 22, 2013).

Chapter 1: Restoring Play to Childhood

7 Regina Milteer and Kenneth Ginsburg, "The Importance of Play in Promoting Healthy Child Development and Maintaining Strong Parent-Child Bond: Focus on Children in Poverty." This article appeared as a policy statement of the American Academy of Pediatrics in its journal, *Pediatrics*, Volume 129, Issue 1 (2012). See: http://pediatrics.aappublications.org/content/129/1/e204.full (accessed June 26, 2013).

8 Sandra Hofferth, "American Children's Outdoor and Indoor Leisure Time," in Elizabeth Goodenough (Ed.), *A Place for Play*, University of Michigan Press (Ann Arbor, MI: 2008), pp. 41-44.

9 See endnote 5.

10 See: http://usplaycoalition.clemson.edu (accessed 7.15.13).

11 See: http://kaboom.org/take_action/playful_city_usa and letter from Darell Hammond, CEO of KaBOOM! to Ray Miller, Mayor of Brisbane California, announcing its recognition as a playful city http://www.brisbaneca.org/news/2013-05-07/brisbane-named-playful-city (Web sites accessed July 1, 2013).

12 See: http://www.letsmove.gov/get-active (accessed July 15, 2013).

13 Centers for Disease Control and Prevention, *The Association Between School-Based Physical Activity, Including Physical Education, and Academic Performance*, U.S. Department of Health and Human Services (Atlanta, GA: 2010) p. 7, at www.cdc.gov/healthyyouth/health_and_academics/pdf/pa-pe_paper.pdf (accessed July 1, 2013).

14 American Academy of Pediatrics Policy Statement, "The Crucial Role of Recess in School," *Pediatrics*, Volume 131, Issue 1, (2013), pp.183-188, at http://pediatrics.aappublications.org/content/131/1/183.full (accessed July 1, 2013).

15 See: http://www.nwf.org/what-we-do/kids-and-nature/policy/ranger-rick-restores-recess.aspx (accessed July 15, 2013).

16 See: http://www.childrenmuseum.org/documents/RecessResourceSheet.pdf (accessed July 15, 2013).

17 Document to be completed in fall 2013. It will be posted at http://usplaycoalition.clemson.edu.

18 Play Wales, "Playing and Hanging Out," at http://www.playwales.org.uk/eng/playinghangingout (accessed July 15, 2013).

19 Amanda Erickson, "The Dumps, Train Tracks, and Polluted Waters Where Kids Play," Dec. 4, 2012, at http://www.theatlanticcities.com/arts-and-lifestyle/2012/12/dumps-train-tracks-and-polluted-water-where-kids-play/4064/ (accessed July 15, 2013).

20 Joe L. Frost, *A History of Children's Play and Environments: Toward a contemporary child-saving movement*, Routledge (New York: 2009) p. 60.

21 Fraser Brown and Sophie Webb, "Children without play," *Journal of Education*, No. 35, (2005), pp. 139-158, at http://dbnweb2.ukzn.ac.za/joe/JoEPDFs/joe%2035%20brown%20and%20webb.pdf (accessed May 22, 2013).

22 Ibid.

23 Ben Shaw, Ben Watson, Björn Frauendienst, Andreas Redecker, and Tim Jones, with Mayer Hillman, "Children's Independent Mobility: a comparative study in England and Germany (1971-2010)" Policy Studies Institute, (London: 2013), at http://www.psi.org.uk/site/news_article/851 (accessed July 15, 2013).

24 *The New York Sun* is now defunct, but Skenazy's description of her child's adventure can be found at http://theweek.com/article/index/96342/the-last-word-advice-from-americas-worst-mom (accessed April 17, 2013).

25 Lenore Skenazy, *Free-Range Kids: How to raise safe, self-reliant children (without going nuts with worry)*, Jossey-Boss (San Francisco: 2009) p. 5.

26 Kristen Laine, "Room to Roam," *AMC Outdoors*, (February 2013), at http://www.outdoors.org/publications/outdoors/2012/kids/free-range-kids.cfm (accessed July 1, 2013).

27 For information about Joe Frost, see Kay Randall's feature story "Child's Play: Demise of play bodes ill for healthy child development, researcher says," The University of Texas at Austin, (2007), at: https://www.utexas.edu/features/2007/playgrounds/index.html (accessed July 15, 2013).

28 See: http://www.cdc.gov/HealthyYouth/obesity/facts.htm (accessed July 2, 2013).

29 Kenneth Ginsburg and others, "The Importance of Play in Promoting Healthy Child Development and Maintaining Strong Parent-Child Bonds," *Pediatrics*, Volume 119, Issue 1 (2007) pp. 182-191. http://pediatrics.aappublications.org/content/119/1/182.full (accessed July 2, 2013).

30 Regina Milteer and Kenneth Ginsburg, op. cit.

31 Kenneth Ginsburg and others, op. cit. See section entitled "Benefits of Play."

32 Ibid.

Chapter 2: Understanding Risk and Its Role in Play

33 The Play Safety Forum, "Managing Risk in Play Provision: A position statement," reprint of 2002 statement by the National Children's Bureau for Play England, (2008), p. 1, at http://www.playengland.org.uk/media/120462/managing-risk-play-safety-forum.pdf. See also: http://www.playengland.org.uk/resources/managing-risk-in-play-provision-a-position-statement.aspx. Related documents include an implementation guide and a briefing for risk managers. (Web sites last accessed July 2, 2013.)

34 For an example, see http://museums-now.blogspot.com/2010/09/when-is-climber-more-than-just-place-to.html (accessed July 2, 2013).

35 For more information on parkour, see https://en.wikipedia.org/wiki/Parkour (accessed April 10, 2013).

36 Examples of extreme sports can be seen at http://extremefreestyle.wordpress.com/2008/05/24/list-of-extreme-sports/ (accessed April 10, 2013).

37 Eleanor J. Gibson and Richard D. Walk, "The 'Visual Cliff,'" *Scientific American*, 202 (1960), pp. 64-71. Also, see: http://psychology.about.com/od/vindex/f/visual-cliff.htm (accessed July 2, 2013).

38 Telephone interview with Danielle Marshall by Halcyon Reese-Learned, April 27, 2009.

39 Jean Liedloff, *The Continuum Concept: In Search of Happiness Lost*, DeCapo Press (Boston: 1975). For more information about Jean Liedloff see her obituary in *The Guardian* at http://www.guardian.co.uk/lifeandstyle/2011/apr/11/jean-liedloff-obituary (accessed May 18, 2013).

40 Touch the Future's motto is "Child development is dependent on adult development." See: http://www.ttfuture.org (accessed May 18, 2013).

41 Jean Liedloff, "The Continuum Concept: Allowing Human Nature to Work Successfully," an interview with Michael Mendizza, p. 8, at http://ttfuture.org/files/2/members/int_leidloff.pdf (accessed May 18, 2013).

42 From an email correspondence on May 17, 2013.

43 Big Lottery Fund Research, Issue 69, "Children's Play: Case study publication," (UK: 2012), p. 5, at http://www.biglotteryfund.org.uk/research/children-and-young-people/-/media/Files/Publication%20Documents/er_eval_cplay_cs.ashx

44 John Tierney, "Can a Playground Be Too Safe?", *The New York Times*, July 18, 2011, at http://www.nytimes.com/2011/07/19/science/19tierney.html?_r=0 (accessed March 25, 2013).

45 Ellen Sandseter and Ellen Beate Hansen, "Categorising risky play—how can we identify risk-taking in children's play?" *European Early Childhood Education Research Journal*, Volume 15, Issue 2, (2007), pp. 237-252.

46 See: http://www.ci.berkeley.ca.us/adventureplayground/

47 Kristin Wiederholt, "Adventure Playgrounds, a Dying Breed," NPR interview of Denise Brown from Berkeley's Adventure Playground, March 9, 2006, at http://www.npr.org/templates/story/story.php?storyId=5254026 (accessed June 26, 2013).

48 See: http://www.ci.berkeley.ca.us/contentdisplay.aspx?id=8656 (last accessed July 2, 2013).

49 Web site for the Huntington Beach Adventure Playground, at http://www.huntingtonbeachca.gov/residents/parks_facilities/parks/huntington_central_park/adventure_playground.cfm

50 Telephone interview with Dottie Hughes by Halcyon Reese-Learned, 2009.

51 See Resources list of this publication for materials by Penny Wilson.

52 As noted by the author, who was present for the training, which was sponsored by the Alliance for Childhood.

53 Telephone interview with Joe Modrich by Halcyon Reese-Learned, February 9, 2009.

54 Deborah J. Leong and Elena Bodrova, "Pioneers In Our Field: Lev Vygotsky—Playing to Learn," at http://www.scholastic.com/teachers/article/pioneers-our-field-lev-vygotsky-playing-learn (accessed December 18, 2012).

55 Bob Hughes, *Play Types: Speculations and Possibilities*, London Centre for Playwork Education and Training, (London: 2006), pp. 50-53.

56 Ibid, pp. 41-42.

57 Ibid, pp. 35-61. For an abbreviated description of Bob Hughes' 16 types of play see Penny Wilson, *The Playwork Primer*, Alliance for Childhood, (College Park, MD: 2010), pp. 22-24, at www.alliance-forchildhood.org/publications (accessed February 5, 2013).

58 Stephen J. Smith, *Risk and Our Pedagogical Relation to Children: On the playground and beyond,* State University of New York Press (Albany: 1998), p. 139.

59 Susan Solomon, *American Playgrounds: Revitalizing Community Space,* University Press of New England (Lebanon, NH: 2005), p. 77.

60 For a wonderful article about Lady Allen, see Penny Wilson, "'children are more complicated than kettles.' the life and work of Lady Allen of Hurtwood," at http://theinternationale.com/pennywilson/38-2/ (accessed February 4, 2013). Also, see: Marjory Allen and Mary Nicholson, *Lady Allen of Hurtwood, Memoirs of an Uneducated Lady,* Thames and Hudson, (London: 1975).

61 *The Play and Playground Encyclopedia,* "Lady Allen of Hurtwood." http://www.pgpedia.com/l/lady-allen-hurtwood (accessed July 13, 2013).

62 Susan Solomon, op. cit., pp. 75-76.

63 Amanda Erickson, "The Politics of Playgrounds, A History" *Atlantic Cities,* March 14, 2012, at http://www.theatlanticcities.com/arts-and-lifestyle/2012/03/politics-playgrounds-history/1480/#.UYhZ_gnrxq9.email (accessed May 8, 2013).

64 Susan Solomon, op. cit.

65 See: http://recentamericanplaygrounds.com/?page_id=3 (accessed May 8, 2013).

66 Kay Randall, op. cit.

67 Joe Frost, "The Dissolution of Children's Outdoor Play: Causes and consequences," (2006), at http://www.imaginationplayground.com/images/content/3/0/3000/The-Dissolution-Of-Children-s-Outdoor-Play-Causes-Conseque.pdf (accessed June 26, 2013).

68 Ibid.

Chapter 3: Lessons about Risk from Adventure Playgrounds

69 This quote is cited in this form on many play websites, but the web-based *Play and Playground Encyclopedia* (http://www.pgpedia.com/l/lady-allen-hurtwood) attributes the quote to a *Time* magazine article written when Lady Allen was touring playgrounds in the US. According to the *Encyclopedia,* when she was asked about American concerns regarding injuries in play, she responded, "It is better to risk a broken leg than a broken spirit. A leg can always mend. A spirit may not." Originally from: "Recreation: Junkyard Playgrounds," *Time,* June 25, 1965, at http://www.time.com/time/magazine/article/0,9171,833789,00.html (Web sites accessed July 15, 2013).

70 Joe L. Frost, *A History of Children's Play and Play Environments,* p. 190.

71 Randall, op.cit.

72 Joe Frost, "Evolution of American Playgrounds," *Scholarpedia,* 7(12):30423 (2012), Section 5.1 at http://www.scholarpedia.org/article/Evolution_of_American_Playgrounds (accessed July 16, 2013).

73 Conversation between Patty Donald and Joan Almon at the Berkeley Adventure Playground, about 2008.

74 Adventure Playground "Holzwurm" in Uster, Switzerland. http://www.holzwurm-uster.ch/index.php (accessed June 26, 2013).

75 There are many ways to categorize play. The Alliance for Childhood has published a list of 12 types. http://www.allianceforchildhood.org/sites/allianceforchildhood.org/files/file/12_types_of_play.pdf (accessed July 2, 2013).

76 Joe Frost, "Evolution of American Playgrounds," op. cit., section 5.1, (accessed April 20, 2013).

77 The web site for the Berkeley Adventure Playground is http://www.ci.berkeley.ca.us/contentdisplay.aspx?id=8656

78 Kristin Wiederholt, op. cit.

79 Joe Frost, "Evolution of American Playgrounds," op. cit.

80 From a report by Halcyon-Reese Learned, Ph.D., commissioned by the Alliance for Childhood.

81 Penny Wilson, *The Playwork Primer,* op. cit., p. 17.

82 See endnote 74.

83 See: http://publicworkshop.us/about/ (accessed July 2, 2013).

84 See: http://publicworkshop.us/blog/2012/11/30/it-would-be-great-if-this-happened-all-over-philly-how-about-adventure-playgrounds-outdoor-tinkering-spaceseverywhere/ (accessed July 16, 2013).

85 See: http://publicworkshop.us/blog/2011/06/20/berlin-researching-temporary-land-use-policy-playgrounds/ (accessed July 16, 2013).

86 Lia Sutton, "Adventure Playgrounds: A children's world in the city," at http://adventureplaygrounds.hampshire.edu/afternoon.html (accessed July 16, 2013).

87 Alice McLerran and Barbara Cooney, *Roxaboxen,* HarperCollins Children's Books, (New York: 1991).

88 Alice McLerran, *The Legacy of Roxaboxen: A collection of voices,* Absey and Company, (Spring, TX: 1998), p. 50.

89 The city of Yuma, Arizona, now owns the hill and has preserved Roxaboxen as a natural desert park, where children still build and play. See: http://www.ci.yuma.az.us/4761.htm (accessed July 16, 2013).

Chapter 4: Injury Rates Relatively Low for Adventure Playgrounds

90 Peter Heseltine, "Inspecting Children's Playgrounds," in Fraser Brown (Ed.), *Playwork: Theory and practice,* Open University Press (Philadelphia: 2003) p. 123. Quoted by Joe Frost, "The Dissolution of Children's Outdoor Play," op. cit., p. 5, (accessed April 20, 2013).

91 See: http://www.londonplay.org.uk/file/1089.pdf (accessed April 20, 2013).

92 Paul Wilkinson and Robert Lockhart, "Safety in Children's Formal Play Environments," a report prepared for the Creative Play Committee of the Ontario Recreation Society and for the Ontario Ministry of Culture and Recreation, Toronto, 1976, at http://www.lin.ca/Files/2352/jk42.htm. Quote is originally from "Case studies," in *Creative Play Resources Bank,* Ontario Ministry of Community and Social Services, 1972.

93 See: http://www.cdc.gov/HomeandRecreationalSafety/Playground-Injuries/playgroundinjuries-factsheet.htm (accessed July 16, 2013)

94 Telephone interview with Joe Frost by Halcyon Reese-Learned, August 15, 2008.

95 Telephone interview with Pam Autio, Program Director, Houston Adventure Play Association by Halcyon Reese-Learned, April 30, 2009, and email correspondence, May, 2013.

96 Telephone interview with Patty Donald by Halcyon Reese-Learned, 2009.

97 Susan Solomon, op. cit., p. 76.

98 Telephone interview with Mayor Tom Bates of the City of Berkeley by Halcyon Reese-Learned, January 21, 2011.

99 See statistics from National Safe Kids Campaign and American Academy of Pediatrics at http://www.lpch.org/DiseaseHealthInfo/HealthLibrary/orthopaedics/stats.html%20 (accessed July 16, 2013).

100 See: http://www.asirt.org/KnowBeforeYouGo/RoadSafetyFacts/RoadCrashStatistics/tabid/213/Default.aspx (accessed July 16, 2013).

Chapter 5: Managing Risk

101 The Play Safety Forum, op. cit.

102 See: http://compliance.berkeley.edu/responsibilities-guide/insurance (accessed July 1, 2013).

103 See: http://popupadventureplay.org/ (accessed July 16, 2013).

104 Suzanna Law, from her presentation at an IPA/USA conference in Atlanta in 2010. (IPA/USA is a branch of the International Play Association and is also known as the American Association for the Child's Right to Play.

105 David Ball, Tim Gill, and Bernard Spiegal, *Managing Risk in Play Provision: Implementation guide*, Play England. See: http://www.freeplaynetwork.org.uk/pubs/risk.pdf (accessed July 16, 2013).

106 From the adventure play "how-to manual" of the Huntington Park adventure play program, p. 10 (no longer in print or on-line).

107 Telephone interview with Dottie Hughes by Halcyon Reese-Learned, 2009.

108 Telephone interview with Bill Sellin by Halcyon Reese-Learned, February 13, 2009.

109 Ibid.

110 Bill Vance, "U. S. Adventure Playground Report," American Adventure Playground Association (San Francisco: 1979), p. 25.

Chapter 6: Next Steps

111 Edward Miller and Joan Almon, *Crisis in the Kindergarten: Why Children Need to Play in School*, Alliance for Childhood, (College Park, MD: 2009), p. 55, at www.allianceforchildhood.org/publications (accessed July 30, 2013).

112 See: www.citymuseum.org/site/ (accessed May 8, 2013).

113 See: http://kaboom.org/blog/our_favorite_dangerous_playgrounds (accessed May 8, 2013).

114 See: http://kaboom.org/blog/playgrounds_made_junk (accessed May 8, 2013).

115 For the full text of the CRC, see http://www.crin.org/docs/resources/treaties/uncrc.asp (accessed May 8, 2013).

116 Tim Gill, *No Fear: Growing up in risk-adverse society*, Calouste Gulbenkian Foundation (London: 2009), p. 19.

117 David Hawkins and Karen Payne, "Wild Zones: Nurturing a generation of children who love the earth and love their own lives," a PowerPoint.

118 Julie Nicholson, P.M. Shimpi, C.T. Carducci, & J.A. Kurnik, "Children's Right to Be Heard: Learning from children about their perspectives on play across the lifespan," (2013). Manuscript submitted for publication. Quotes are from an email from Julie Nicholson to Joan Almon on May 9, 2013. (Punctuation, age, and gender of children are rephrased in the quotes for ease of reading.)

119 Conversation with Christine Chen by Joan Almon on April 17, 2013, in Washington, D.C.

120 Liza Sullivan, "My Family's Park-a-Day Summer Challenge." See: http://kaboom.org/docs/documents/pdf/Liza-Winnetka-Alliance.pdf (accessed May 8, 2013).

121 See Mike Lanza's blog about play in the neighborhood at www.playborhood.com (accessed July 16, 2013). See also Pop-Up Adventure Play and Wild-Zones in the Resource section.

122 The Children and Nature Network has created an online toolkit entitled "Nature Clubs for Families," available at http://www.childrenandnature.org/downloads/NCFF_toolkit2.pdf (accessed May 8, 2013).

123 Sign up for free updates about play at www.allianceforchildhood.org and http://usplaycoalition.clemson.edu/

124 See: http://kaboom.org/take_action/playful_city_us

Resources

Adventure playgrounds in the U.S.:

Berkeley, CA Adventure Playground
http://www.ci.berkeley.ca.us/
ContentDisplay.aspx?id=8656

Huntington Beach, CA Adventure Playground
http://www.huntingtonbeachca.gov/Residents/Parks_
Facilities/parks/huntington_central_park/Adventure_
Playground.cfm

Yorba Linda, CA adventure play camps
http://www.ocregister.com/articles/campers-366851-
playground-adventure.html

Mercer Island, WA adventure playground
http://www.mercergov.org/Page.asp?NavID=2768

Adventure playgrounds in the U.K., a sampling:

Glamis Adventure Playground in the East End of
London. A video interview with play expert Bernard
Spiegel. Filmed by Kristin Eno of Little Creatures Film
Company, NY, vimeo.com/29645438

The Land, an adventure playground in North Wales.
U.S. filmmaker Erin Davis is developing a documentary,
and a trailer can be seen at http://playfreemovie.com/
trailer2/. A radio program by Erin Davis, "Of Kith and
Kids," can be heard at http://transom.org/?p=37317

"Adventure Playgrounds," a video by the
National Playing Fields Association. A Stanley
Schofield Production on YouTube at
http://www.youtube.com/watch?v=Uwj1wh5k5PY

Play in the U.K., a few of many excellent sites:

Ip-dip, www.ip-dip.com
A free, email newsletter about play and playwork

London Play, www.londonplay.org.uk
Many resources including books on adventure
playgrounds and playwork

Play England, www.playengland.org.uk
An excellent source of play publications including
"Managing Risk in Play Provision" and "Adventure
Playgrounds: Built by communities"

Play Wales, www.playwales.org.uk/eng
Resources include "The Venture: a case study of an
adventure playground" and an information sheet,
"Play and Challenge"

Alliance for Childhood, www.allianceforchildhood.org
The Alliance focuses on restoring play to children's lives
and related issues, publishes a monthly update, and
has a number of publications and videos that can be
found on the website's publication page.

Fraser Brown, director of degree programs in playwork
at Leeds Metropolitan University in England.
Author of several books on playwork, including
Foundations of Playwork.

Joe Frost, professor emeritus from U.T. Austin and a
leading U.S. authority on play and playgrounds. He has
authored many books including *The Developmental
Benefits of Playgrounds*.

Tim Gill, a leading author and blogger on play and risk
in the U.K. He is author of *No Fear: Growing up in a
risk-averse society* (available on-line at
www.gulbenkian.org.uk) and blogger of "Rethinking
Childhood" at http://rethinkingchildhood.com

Elizabeth Goodenough, educator and advocate for play,
was consultant for the PBS documentary "Where Do
the Children Play?" and is editor of the books *Where
Do the Children Play?*, *A Place for Play*, and *Secret
Spaces of Childhood* (all available from University of
Michigan Press).

International Play Association, www.ipausa.org
Promotes play and the child's right to play

KaBOOM!, www.kaboom.org
Helps communities build playgrounds, advocates for

play, publishes reports, and creates videos, including "The Benefits of Risk in Children's Play."

Lady Allen of Hurtwood, advocate for children's play and a founder of adventure playgrounds in England. Her classic book, *Planning for Play*, is available on-line at www.play-scapes.com. An archival film of her speaking about the inclusive playground she developed in Chelsea can be found at the bottom of the page at http://transom.org/?p=37317.

Play and Playground Encyclopedia, www.pgpedia.com

Pop-Up Adventure Play, http://popupadventureplaygrounds.wordpress.com

PlayScapes, http://www.play-scapes.com
A blog and source for classic books on playground design

Lenore Skenazy, author of *Free-Range Kids*

Susan Solomon, author of *American Playgrounds: Revitalizing Community Space*

Lia Sutton, photographer of adventure playgrounds, www.liasutton.com

U.S. Play Coalition, http://usplaycoalition.clemson.edu
A national play coalition that offers free membership, a monthly play update, and an annual conference at Clemson University in S.C.

Wild-Zones, www.wild-zone.net

Penny Wilson, London-based playworker
Author of *The Playwork Primer* and featured in the video "Playwork: An Introduction" (both available at www.allianceforchildhood.org/publications)

About the author

Joan Almon is Director of Programs at the U.S. Alliance for Childhood, which she co-founded in 1999. She gives lectures and workshops on child development and play, and has authored many articles and book chapters. She was formerly a Waldorf early childhood educator and has been a consultant to schools around the world. Her favorite activities include story telling and puppetry, and relaxing with family in a 150-year-old log house in the mountains of Tennessee.

The Land, Wales

Acknowledgements

Copy editor: Colleen Cordes
Graphic designer: Niki Matsoukas
Front and back cover photos: © photosearch.com